The Symbols of Christmas
The Story of Jesus Christ

By Robert Adams

Tate Publishing, LLC

Published in the United States of America
By TATE PUBLISHING, LLC
All rights reserved.
Do not duplicate without permission.

Unless otherwise identified, Scripture quotations in this book are from The Holy Bible, New King James Version, original work copyright © 1979, 1980, 1982 by Thomas Nelson, Inc., Nashville, Tennessee.
All rights reserved.

Book Design by TATE PUBLISHING, LLC.

Printed in the United States of America by
TATE PUBLISHING, LLC
127 East Trade Center Terrace
Mustang, OK 73064
(888) 361-9473

Publisher's Cataloging in Publication

Adams, Robert

The Symbols of Christmas / Robert Adams

Originally published in Mustang, OK: TATE PUBLISHING: 2004

1. Christmas   2. Children / Evangelism

ISBN 1-9331480-5-5 $18.95

Copyright 2004

First Printing: November 2004

*This book is dedicated first and foremost
to my Lord and Savior,*
Jesus Christ.
*I pray that it will bring glory, honor, and praise to His Holy Name.
Words seem so inadequate to tell you, Jesus, how much I love You.*

I take this time to also dedicate it to my wife,
Karen,
*for all the love, encouragement, and support she has given me
all of our years together, especially with this project.*

I wish to thank my three sons:
Brent, Brandon, and Brock
*for believing in me.
I thank you that I never heard you complain about
having a father called into the ministry.
God truly has blessed me with three wonderful sons
who have encouraged me with love and faith.*

Mom and Dad,
*thank you for the early teaching and example of loving God.
Your devotion and adoration of the Lord has always been
an inspiration to me.*

Foreword

In 35 years of ministry, I have been privileged to meet numerous individuals who are committed to the Lordship of Jesus Christ. Their relationship is solid and they get excited talking about and living for our Lord.

In 1984, while traveling with my family doing Gospel Music Concerts and Evangelism in churches across America, I encountered such a person in the Oklahoma City area, and it was one of those instant bonds that you knew would last for a long time. Robert Adams and his wife Karen became dear friends and our relationship has been one of mutual love and respect.

When you hear and now read what Robert has to say, you find that he has a keen insight into the Word of God and is a man of God with a commitment to Bible study and prayer. It is through this study and prayer that the exciting words of this book have become a life-giving influence to children of all ages.

The power of the Word is sharp and effective. It is also simple and exciting.

The worldly symbols of Christmas, so long used by Satan to effectively distract from the Christmas story, have at last been retrieved for the Kingdom of God. These symbols have been rendered powerless to Satan and all-powerful for the Gospel of Jesus Christ. God wants to convey great truth to you and help you help your children and grandchildren.

The Scriptures remind us "unless we become as one of these little ones, we will not inherit the Kingdom of God." Books that talk about God so that a child can understand and be inspired are at a premium. They are few and far between. It is for this time that Robert has taken seriously this venture and committed his life to help us train up our children in the way they should go.

There are children everywhere ready to celebrate Christmas, ready to shout praises to God and ready to live a life the way God intended, "more than a conqueror."

The Symbols of Christmas as presented by Robert Adams is an incredible story of Jesus Christ. Read this book with confidence and be blessed.

Darrell Geist, Pastor
Lighthouse Community Church
Downs, Kansas

Introduction

This is important for all parents to read and understand how we can become **"more than conquerors"** during the Christmas season.

What is Christmas? Is it anything important at all?

To begin with, we must understand that all the importance of Christmas is not contained in:

THE DATE (December 25)—The date came from a pagan observance of the birthday of the unconquered sun. During this time, the pagans held two weeks of feasts, parades, special music, gift giving, lighted candles, and green trees. The holiday was Christianized, and in 336 AD Emperor Constantine declared Christ's birthday an official Roman holiday. However, we do not really know when Jesus was born. The date has nothing to do with Scripture.

THE NAME—"Christmas" is a short form of Christ Mass, a Catholic Mass that grew out of a specific feast day established in 1038 AD called "Christi's Masse." It has nothing to do with Scripture.

SANTA CLAUS—The idea of Santa Claus is the result of a fourth century bishop's activity. His name was St. Nicholas and he gave his possessions to the poor, and supposedly brought back to life two dead children. Thus, he was a giver of gifts who was particularly important to children. St. Nicholas was important in Holland, but eventually Clement Moore in his poem "The Night Before Christmas" (published in 1823) perpetuated the idea in America.

THE CARDS—Christmas cards started less than 100 years ago. This year over $900 million will be spent on Christmas cards and over $400 million to mail them.

THE SPIRIT OF GIVING—In modern-day America it is more the spirit of indulgence. Over $12 billion will be spent on 7 billion gifts, all wrapped in $950 million worth of paper.

THE TREE—The tree did not arrive until the 16th century. Martin Luther was the first person to have a lighted tree.

HOW MUCH OF CHRISTMAS IS CHRISTIAN? NONE OF IT! None of it is biblical, the Lord commands none of it, none of it is apostolic, and the early church never observed any of it!

One must remember that God is in control and satan cannot do anything without God's knowledge. Take for example the shepherd's that were chosen to hear the angel's announcement of the Savior's birth. Why were they chosen? They were chosen because only one group of shepherds raised the temple flock. They were the ones who raised the Passover Lamb. They cared for the lamb that would be slain for the sins of

Israel. This perfect lamb's blood would be sprinkled in the Holy of Holies. Only these shepherd's would know the significance of the angel's words, "And this will be the sign to you: You will find a Babe wrapped in swaddling cloths, lying in a manger (Luke 2:12)." You see they also separated the ewe from the rest of the flock when it came time for her to give birth to the lamb. They did this so nothing would blemish the lamb. As the lamb was born, they cradled him in their hands and cleaned him up. Then they would wrap the lamb in swaddling clothes (tight binding strips of cloth). After wrapping the lamb up, they would place him in straw of cut grass. The lamb would kick against the tight binding cloth trying to get up, thus strengthening his legs. So after a short time the tight binding clothes would be removed and he would be strong enough to stand and nurse without falling and becoming bruised or cut. They were the only ones to understand "This will be a sign to you." They knew to look for Him on the outskirts of Bethlehem.

Romans 8:37 Yet in all these things we are more than conquerors through Him who loved us.

Now to be more than a conqueror is not merely to put down the enemy, but to rise to higher heights upon his prostrate form. To be more than conqueror is not only to withstand the blows of the weapons in the enemy's hand, but also to seize these same weapons and use them in an aggressive attack upon the enemy. The Romans used this phrase when referring to a special warrior who was able to use his enemy's strategy and weapons against him to win the victory.

So let us take the holiday that the world and satan have tried to destroy with commercialization, rush, depression, and nervous tension and use the ***Symbols*** that are here for and to the glory of God. Let us take satan's weapons and his strategy and use them against him. What he brought about to destroy the gospel message, we will use to tell the glorious story of the birth, life, death, and resurrection of our Lord and Savior Jesus Christ.

This sermon has been preached every year since Christmas of 1974 and this book is being written in hopes that parents, churches, children workers, or anyone who wants to be "**more than a conqueror**" will use this as a teaching tool for their children, family, and friends. If anyone is taught or if anyone reads this every Christmas as they decorate the house for the Christmas holidays, then they (especially a child) will always think about God's love and Jesus every time they see the decorations. Satan's plan will have been defeated and each person who tells the gospel story with the **"Symbols of Christmas"** will become "**more than conquerors through Jesus Christ**."

Looking Inside...

Christmas Bells

Red Poinsettia

The Christmas Wreath

The Christmas Gift

Opening Christmas Gifts

Children and Christmas

The Holly Decorations

The Twinkling Lights

The Evergreen Tree

The Stocking

The Mistletoe

The Turtle Dove

Candy Cane

Santa Claus

The Reindeer

The Sleigh

The Elves

My Christmas Prayer

Christmas Bells

The Christmas bells should remind one of the Good News about the birth of our dear Savior that was heralded by the angels about 2,000 years ago.

> *Luke 2:9–12 (9) And behold, an angel of the Lord stood before them, and the glory of the Lord shone around them, and they were greatly afraid. (10) Then the angel said to them, "Do not be afraid, for behold, I bring you good tidings of great joy which will be to all people. (11) For there is born to you this day in the city of David a Savior, who is Christ the Lord. (12) And this will be the sign to you: You will find a Babe wrapped in swaddling cloths, lying in a manger."*

The bells should remind Americans about freedom since we have the Liberty Bell that was made to celebrate our independence as a nation. We should be reminded of the liberty we gained by Jesus who came and lived, died, and was resurrected to give us freedom from sin and bondage.

> *Galatians 5:1 Stand fast therefore in the liberty by which Christ has made us free, and do not be entangled again with a yoke of bondage.*

The bells should remind us about the warning of how those who miss the gift of God's Son will one day spend an eternity in hell.

> *Matthew 10:28 And do not fear those who kill the body but cannot kill the soul. But rather fear Him who is able to destroy both soul and body in hell.*

Red Poinsettia

The red of the poinsettia symbolizes the precious blood of Jesus that was shed for you and me on Calvary.

> *Ephesians 1:7 In Him we have redemption through His blood, the forgiveness of sins, according to the riches of His grace.*

The gold or yellow should remind us of the golden streets in Heaven. The place prepared for God's Children; of His crown He left in Glory, and also the golden promises of God's Holy Word.

> *Revelation 21:18, 21 (18) The construction of its wall was of jasper; and the city was pure gold, like clear glass. (21) The twelve gates were twelve pearls: each individual gate was of one pearl. And the street of the city was pure gold, like transparent glass.*

> *Psalms 19:9–11 (9) The fear of the LORD is clean, enduring forever; The judgments of the LORD are true and righteous altogether. (10) More to be desired are they than gold, Yea, than much fine gold; Sweeter also than honey and the honeycomb. (11) Moreover by them Your servant is warned, And in keeping them there is great reward.*

The Christmas Wreath

The wreath is a circle unbroken, which symbolizes that's God's Love, is unbroken.

> *Romans 8:38–39 (38) For I am persuaded that neither death nor life, nor angels nor principalities nor powers, nor things present nor things to come, (39) nor height nor depth, nor any other created thing, shall be able to separate us from the love of God which is in Christ Jesus our Lord.*

It is in the shape of a circle, which means that God's love encircles the world.

> *John 3:16 For God so loved the world that He gave His only begotten Son, that whoever believes in Him should not perish but have everlasting life.*

It has no beginning and no end. Jesus, who is Alpha and the Omega, has no beginning or end.

> *Revelation 21:6 And He [Jesus] said to me, "It is done! I am the Alpha and the Omega, the Beginning and the End. I will give of the fountain of the water of life freely to him who thirsts."*

The Christmas Gifts

The gifts remind us of the Gift that God gave the world, the great Gift of His Son to redeem us from sin.

> *Romans 6:23 For the wages of sin is death, but the gift of God is eternal life in Christ Jesus our Lord.*

The gifts are put under, on, and near a tree, as God's Son was put on a tree and died on that tree to give us the gift of eternal Life.

> *Acts 13:29–30 (29) Now when they had fulfilled all that was written concerning Him, they took Him down from the tree and laid Him in a tomb. (30) But God raised Him from the dead.*

The gifts are wrapped, as was the baby Jesus wrapped in swaddling cloths.

> *Luke 2:12 And this will be the sign to you: You will find a Babe wrapped in swaddling cloths, lying in a manger.*

Opening Christmas Gifts

As we open our gifts under the tree, they bring great joy and delight. Jesus was also taken down from the tree, laid in a tomb, and wrapped in grave clothes. On the Resurrection morn, He arose and the tomb was opened to show the resurrection of Jesus Christ. This gift gives us salvation. Because He lives, I also have eternal life through Him.

> *John 20:1, 5–9 (1)On the first day of the week Mary Magdalene went to the tomb early, while it was still dark, and saw that the stone had been taken away from the tomb. (5) And he, stooping down and looking in, saw the linen cloths lying there; yet he did not go in. (6) Then Simon Peter came, following him, and went into the tomb; and he saw the linen cloths lying there, (7) and the handkerchief that had been around His head, not lying with the linen cloths, but folded together in a place by itself. (8) Then the other disciple, who came to the tomb first, went in also; and he saw and believed. (9) For as yet they did not know the Scripture, that He must rise again from the dead.*

Children and Christmas

Christmas is primarily for the children. They have the excitement, faith, joy, and anticipation. Santa Claus invites children to come and tell him everything that their hearts desire. So Jesus also invites all the children to come to Him and tell Him their heart's desires. He also said we were to become like little children to enter the kingdom of God.

> *Mark 10:14–15 (14) But when Jesus saw it, He was greatly displeased and said to them, "Let the little children come to Me, and do not forbid them; for of such is the kingdom of God. (15) Assuredly, I say to you, whoever does not receive the kingdom of God as a little child will by no means enter it."*

The Holly Decorations

The holly has thorns that remind us of the crown of thorns that Jesus wore for us.

> *John 19:1–2 (1) So then Pilate took Jesus and scourged Him. (2) And the soldiers twisted a crown of thorns and put it on His head, and they put on Him a purple robe.*

The holly berries are red and remind us of the blood that came from His head and body.

> *Colossians 1:13–14 (13) He has delivered us from the power of darkness and conveyed us into the kingdom of the Son of His love, (14) in whom we have redemption through His blood, the forgiveness of sins.*

The holly berries also grow in clusters of three that remind us of the Holy Trinity (Father, Son, and Holy Spirit).

> *Matthew 28:19 Go therefore and make disciples of all the nations, baptizing them in the name of the Father and of the Son and of the Holy Spirit.*

> *John 15:26 But when the Helper comes, whom I shall send to you from the Father, the Spirit of truth who proceeds from the Father, He will testify of Me.*

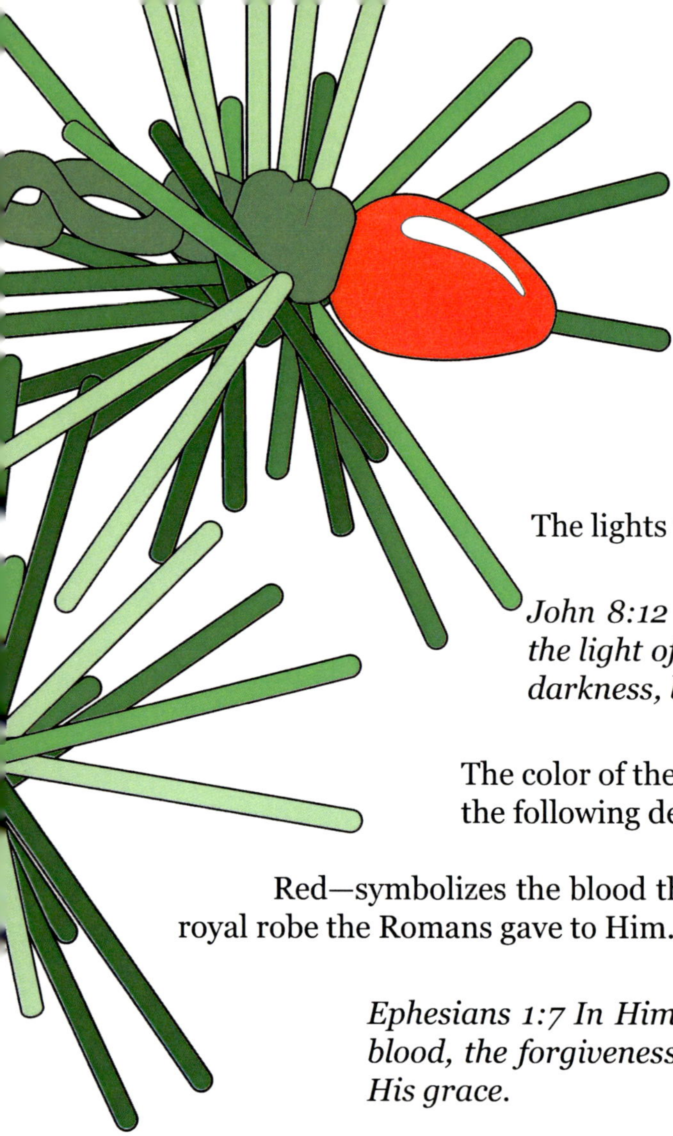

The Twinkling Lights

The lights remind us of the Light of the world—Jesus Christ.

John 8:12 Then Jesus spoke to them again, saying, "I am the light of the world. He who follows Me shall not walk in darkness, but have the light of life."

The color of the lights means something very important too as the following demonstrates:

Red—symbolizes the blood that was shed for all of us on Calvary. And for the royal robe the Romans gave to Him.

Ephesians 1:7 In Him we have redemption through His blood, the forgiveness of sins, according to the riches of His grace.

Blue—the royal heritage that Jesus has and has given to us who believe; and for the heaven that He has ascended to, where He is seated at the right hand of God, and will return from as the KING OF KINGS.

Revelation 17:14 These will make war with the Lamb, and the Lamb will overcome them, for He is Lord of lords and King of kings; and those who are with Him are called, chosen, and faithful.

Revelation 5:9–10 (9) And they sang a new song, saying: "You are worthy to take the scroll, And to open its seals; For You were slain, And have redeemed us to God by Your blood Out of every tribe and tongue and people and nation, (10) And have made us kings and priests to our God; And we shall reign on the earth."

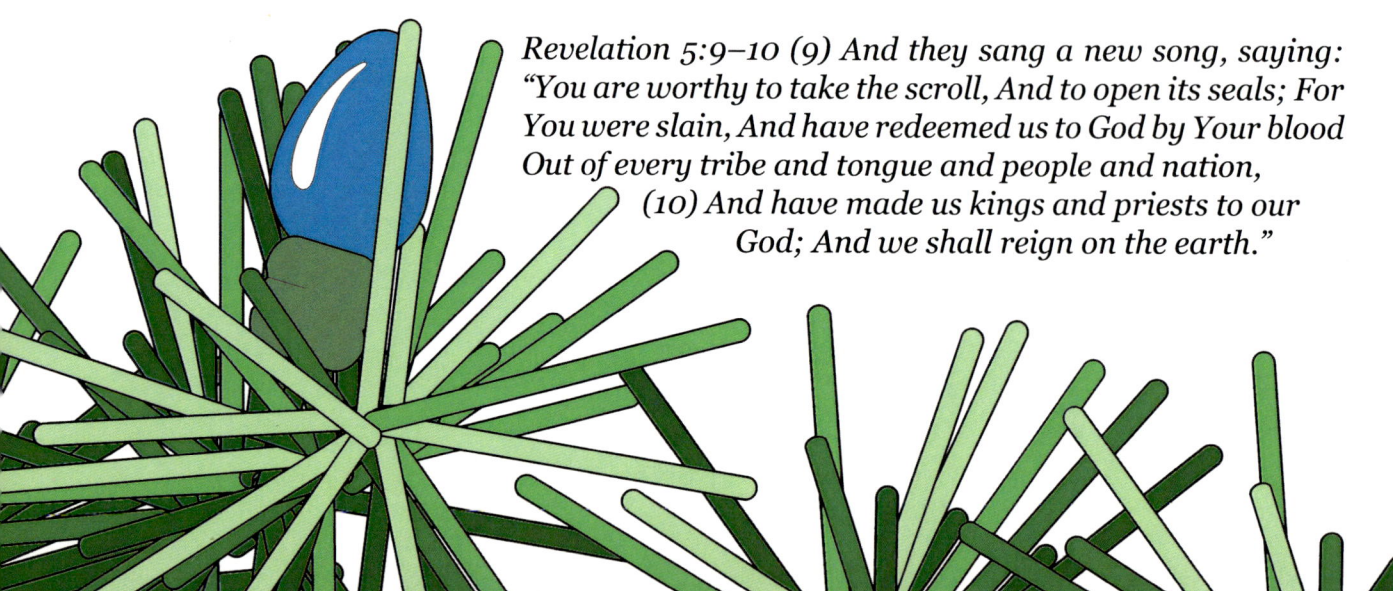

Green—the everlasting presence of the Holy Spirit and the undying love of God for us His creation.

> *1 Corinthians 6:19 Or do you not know that your body is the temple of the Holy Spirit who is in you, whom you have from God, and you are not your own?*

White—for the purity that my sins red like crimson are now white as wool, because of His shed blood.

> *Isaiah 1:18 "Come now, and let us reason together," Says the LORD, "Though your sins are like scarlet, They shall be as white as snow; Though they are red like crimson, They shall be as wool."*

Yellow—for the golden streets in Heaven and what some people refer to as the golden promises of God's Word. Also it should remind us that God considers our measure of faith more precious than gold.

> *Revelation 21:21 The twelve gates were twelve pearls: each individual gate was of one pearl. And the street of the city was pure gold, like transparent glass.*

> *Psalms 119:127 Therefore I love Your commandments More than gold, yes, than fine gold!*

> *1 Peter 1:7 …that the genuineness of your faith, being much more precious than gold that perishes, though it is tested by fire, may be found to praise, honor, and glory at the revelation of Jesus Christ…*

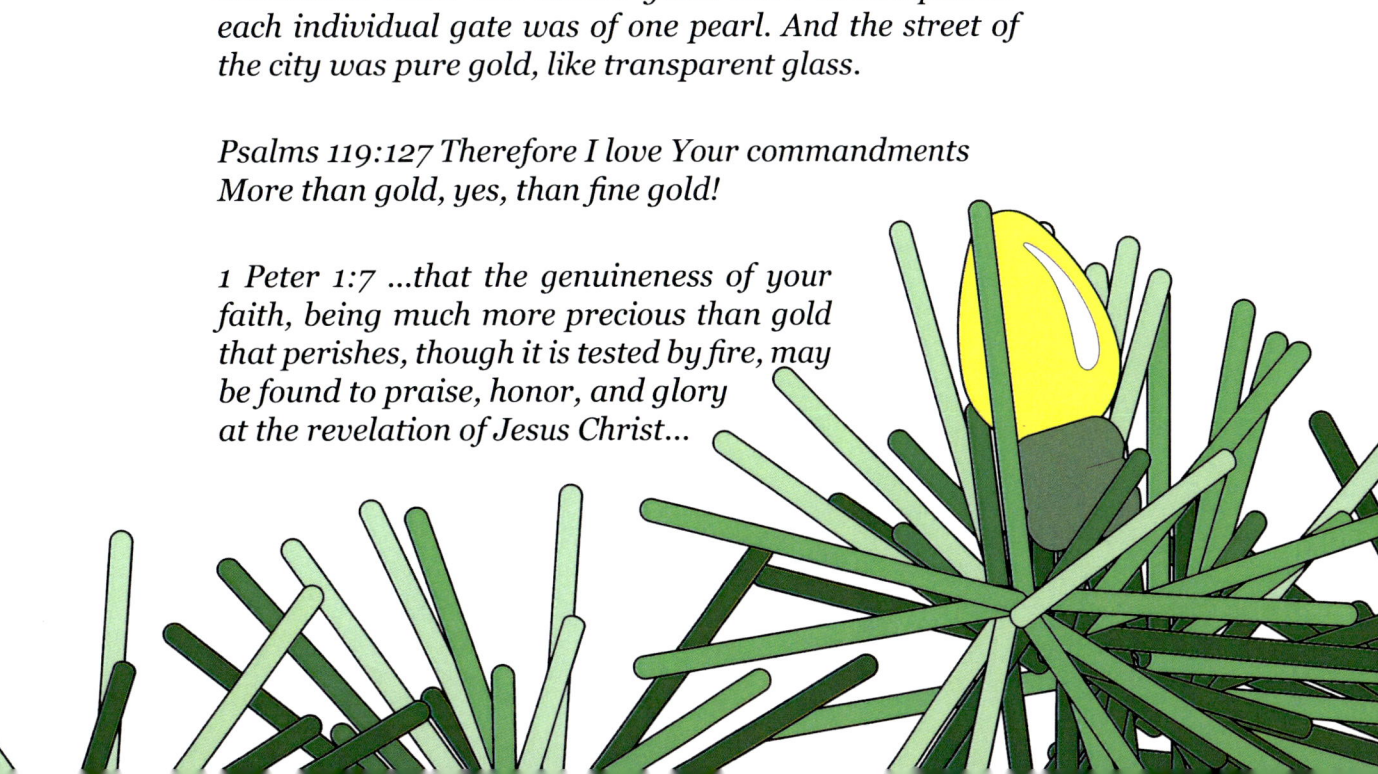

When put on a Christmas tree, the twinkling lights start at the top and spiral down. This represents the blessings of God that come down to us His children. They should also remind us that the Light of the world left Heaven to come to Earth.

> *John 3:13 No one has ascended to heaven but He who came down from heaven, that is, the Son of Man who is in heaven.*

> *John 6:38 For I have come down from heaven, not to do My own will, but the will of Him who sent Me.*

If you are one who starts at the bottom of the Christmas tree and goes upward, this would symbolizes the resurrection of Jesus. This would represent His ascension as the Light of the World returning to heaven and becoming the first fruits of our resurrection.

> *Ephesians 4:9–10 (9) (Now this, "He ascended"—what does it mean but that He also first descended into the lower parts of the earth? (10) He who descended is also the One who ascended far above all the heavens, that He might fill all things.)*

The Evergreen Tree

The evergreen tree is green and fresh from season to season as is the presence and love of God.

> *Psalms 102:27 But You are the same, And Your years will have no end.*

> *Hebrews 13:8 Jesus Christ is the same yesterday, today, and forever.*

The tree reminds us of the everlasting life that we have when we accept the sacrifice of Jesus Christ.

> *Romans 6:23 For the wages of sin is death, but the gift of God is eternal life in Christ Jesus our Lord.*

> *1 John 5:11 And this is the testimony: that God has given us eternal life, and this life is in His Son.*

The tree reminds us that Jesus was crucified on the cross.

> *Acts 10:39–41 (39) And we are witnesses of all things which He did both in the land of the Jews and in Jerusalem, whom they killed by hanging on a tree. (40) Him God raised up on the third day, and showed Him openly, (41) not to all the people, but to witnesses chosen before by God, even to us who ate and drank with Him after He arose from the dead.*

The Stocking

The stocking is filled with small gifts and candy. This symbolizes what some refer to as the small things that God does for each individual, and the Word of God that is full of the sweet promises of God.

An example of the little things would be God helping us to find or remember something that has been misplaced or reading just the right Bible verse for that day or circumstance.

Psalm 119:103 How sweet are Your words to my taste, Sweeter than honey to my mouth!

James 1:17 Every good gift and every perfect gift is from above, and comes down from the Father of lights, with whom there is no variation or shadow of turning.

The Mistletoe

It derives its strength and life from another source; it must be connected to a living tree.

> *John 15:4 Abide in Me, and I in you. As the branch cannot bear fruit of itself, unless it abides in the vine, neither can you, unless you abide in Me.*

We are the same way. He is the vine and we are the branches. We must be connected to Christ to get our strength and stay alive spiritually.

> Christ said, *"Apart from Me you can do nothing."*
> *John 15:5*

The Turtle Dove

Reminds us of the coming of the Holy Spirit to abide within us.

> *John 14:16 And I will pray the Father, and He will give you another Helper, that He may abide with you forever—*

It is a bird of a quiet nature yet remarkable strength and wisdom, as the Holy Spirit is to us (strength and wisdom).

> *John 14:26 But the Helper, the Holy Spirit, whom the Father will send in My name, He will teach you all things, and bring to your remembrance all things that I said to you.*

> *Eph 3:20–21 (20) Now to Him who is able to do exceedingly abundantly above all that we ask or think, according to the power that works in us, (21) to Him be glory in the church by Christ Jesus to all generations, forever and ever. Amen.*

Candy Cane

Again notice the colors:

Red and White—the blood that was shed for our salvation that washes our sins white and pure.

> *Matthew 26:28 For this is My blood of the new covenant, which is shed for many for the remission of sins.*

> *Ephesians 1:7 In Him we have redemption through His blood, the forgiveness of sins, according to the riches of His grace.*

Notice that it is in the shape of a Shepherds staff. Jesus is the Great Shepherd. When turned upside down it looks like the letter "J"—Jesus.

> *John 10:11 I am the good shepherd. The good shepherd gives His life for the sheep.*

Also the peppermint candy comes in a long rod without the crooked end. The rod for the shepherd was an instrument of correction and protection. Just as our Jesus corrects and protects us.

> *Psalms 23:4 Yea, though I walk through the valley of the shadow of death, I will fear no evil; For You are with me; Your rod and Your staff, they comfort me.*

> *Hebrews 12:6 For whom the LORD loves He chastens, And scourges every son whom He receives.*

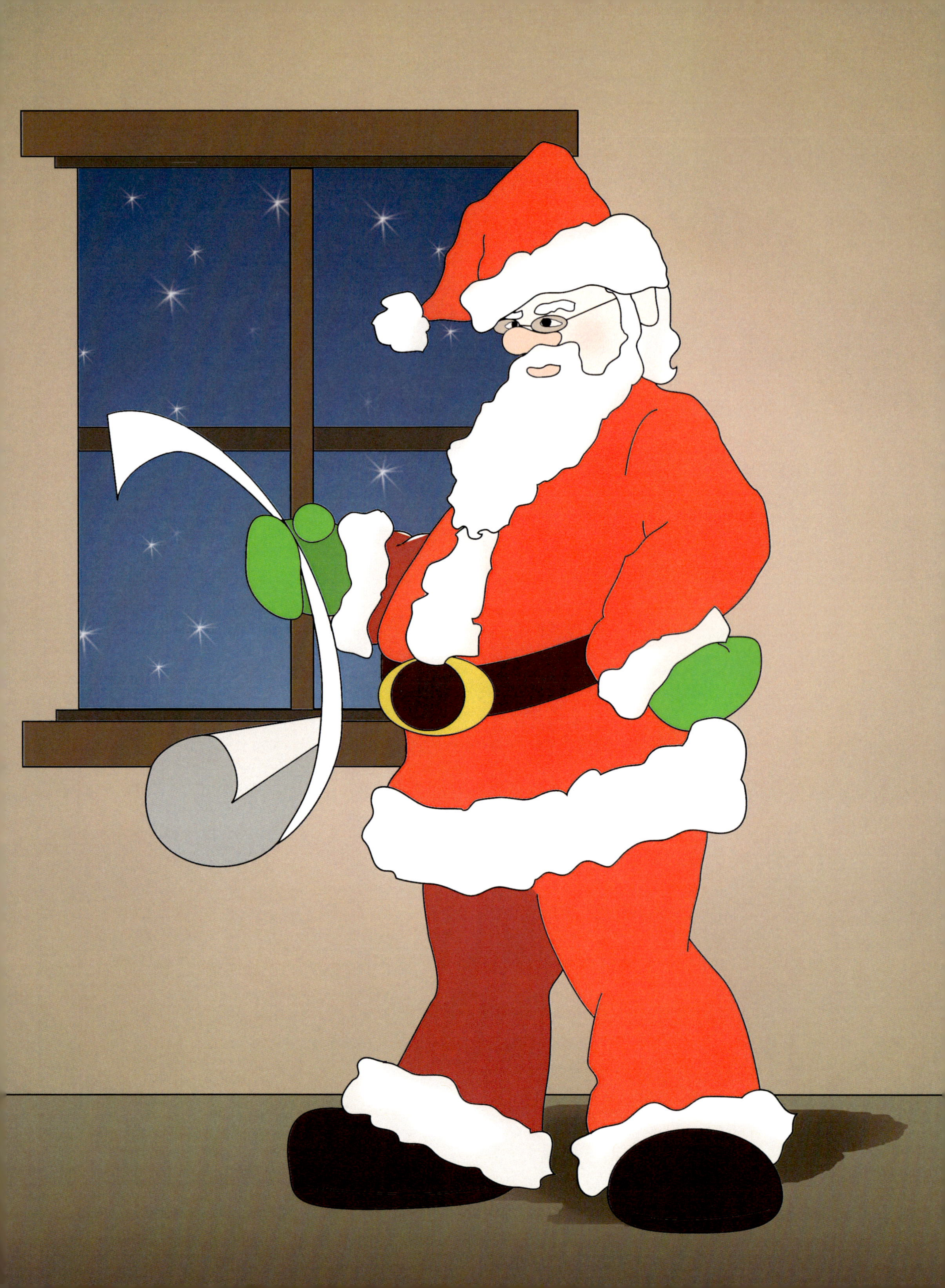

Santa Claus

Even Santa Claus symbolizes the goodness of God. His suit is a bright red color, reminding us again of the shed blood of Jesus.

His belt is black, which reminds us of the nature of sin (black, decaying, death). It encircles him, as sin will do if allowed to reign in one's life.

> *Romans 6:12 Therefore do not let sin reign in your mortal body, that you should obey it in its lusts.*

Underneath the black belt is a patch of red and underneath that is a circle of pure white that also goes all around to show that any where sin goes God's atonement can go and cleanse us clean.

> *1 John 1:7 But if we walk in the light as He is in the light, we have fellowship with one another, and the blood of Jesus Christ His Son cleanses us from all sin.*

No one is supposed to know exactly when Santa Claus will come to bring us the many gifts. No one knows when the Son of Man is coming to reclaim His followers.

> *Mark 13:32–33 (32) But of that day and hour no one knows, not even the angels in heaven, nor the Son, but only the Father. (33) Take heed, watch and pray; for you do not know when the time is.*

He is a jolly man. God wants us to be full of joy for He rejoices over us.

> *John 15:11 These things I have spoken to you, that My joy may remain in you, and that your joy may be full.*

> *Zephaniah 3:17 The LORD your God in your midst, The Mighty one, will save; He will rejoice over you with gladness, He will quiet you with His love, He will rejoice over you with singing.*

The image of the man is the pure essence of the perfect love of God, who gives to all men freely.

> *Romans 8:32 He who did not spare His own Son, but delivered Him up for us all, how shall He not with Him also freely give us all things?*

Just like Santa, God has a list of who is good (righteous) and who is evil (or bad).

> *Revelation 20:15 And anyone not found written in the Book of Life was cast into the lake of fire.*

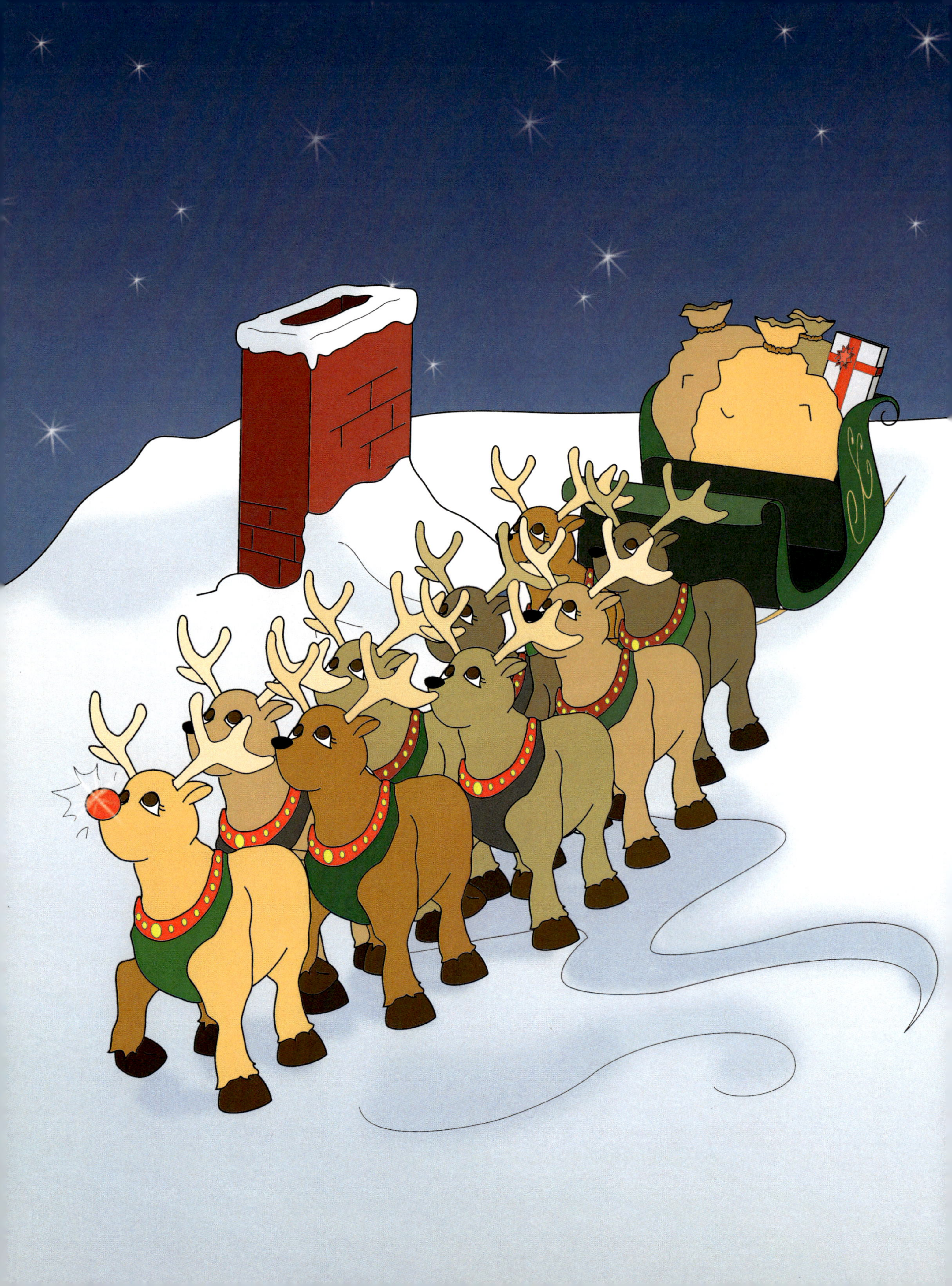

The Reindeer

The reindeer remind us of the angels that came to proclaim the good news of God's gift that came to earth that night. The reindeer bring the love and gifts to those anxiously waiting, just like the angels who heralded the "good news" of the birth of the Messiah, the gift and love of God in human form.

> *Luke 2:13–14 (13) And suddenly there was with the angel a multitude of the heavenly host praising God and saying: (14) "Glory to God in the highest, And on earth peace, goodwill toward men!"*

Rudolph's red nose reminds us that the blood of Christ must lead the way through the blackness of sin.

Rudolph was mocked and ridiculed until he was needed, just as Christ is ridiculed, mocked, and ignored until a person has need of Him.

> *John 14:6 Jesus said to him, "I am the way, the truth, and the life. No one comes to the Father except through Me."*

> *Isaiah 53:3 He is despised and rejected by men, A Man of sorrows and acquainted with grief. And we hid, as it were, our faces from Him; He was despised, and we did not esteem Him.*

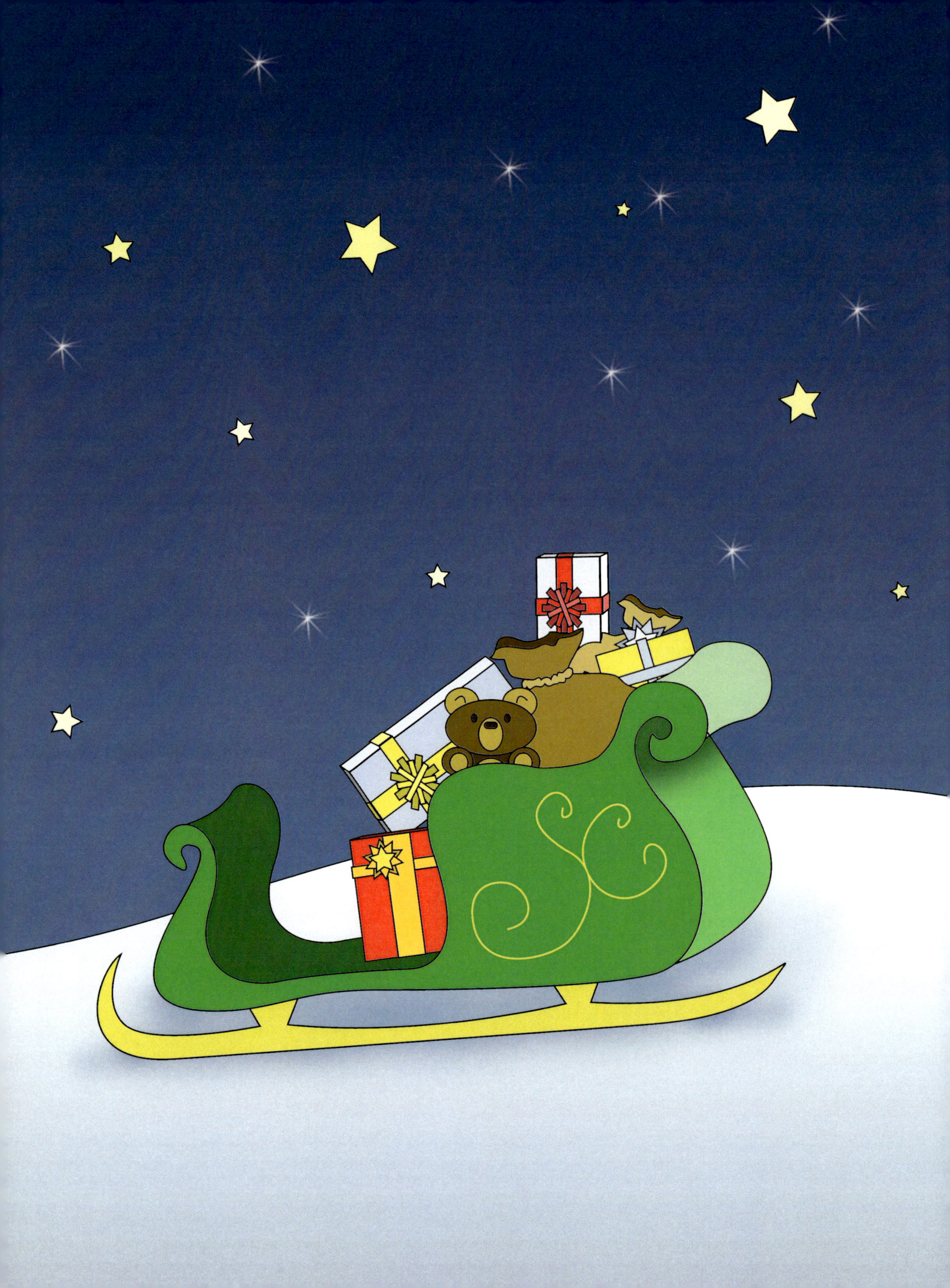
SC

The Sleigh

The sleigh reminds us of the heart of God--ever filled with good things for us, His children.

> *James 1:17 Every good gift and every perfect gift is from above, and comes down from the Father of lights, with whom there is no variation or shadow of turning.*

When you think of Santa's sleigh, you immediately imagine gifts he is bringing. Jesus also ascended so that He could give gifts to His children.

> *Ephesians 4:7–8 (7) But to each one of us grace was given according to the measure of Christ's gift. (8) Therefore He says: "When He ascended on high, He led captivity captive, And gave gifts to men."*

You should be reminded of the great gift that Jesus gave to each one of His children, the gift of the Holy Spirit.

> *Acts 2:38–39 (38) Then Peter said to them, "Repent, and let every one of you be baptized in the name of Jesus Christ for the remission of sins; and you shall receive the gift of the Holy Spirit. (39) For the promise is to you and to your children, and to all who are afar off, as many as the Lord our God will call."*

The greatest gift that God gave to everyone who will accept Jesus as Lord and Savior is eternal life with God.

> *Ephesians 2:8–9 (8) For by grace you have been saved through faith, and that not of yourselves; it is the gift of God, (9) not of works, lest anyone should boast.*

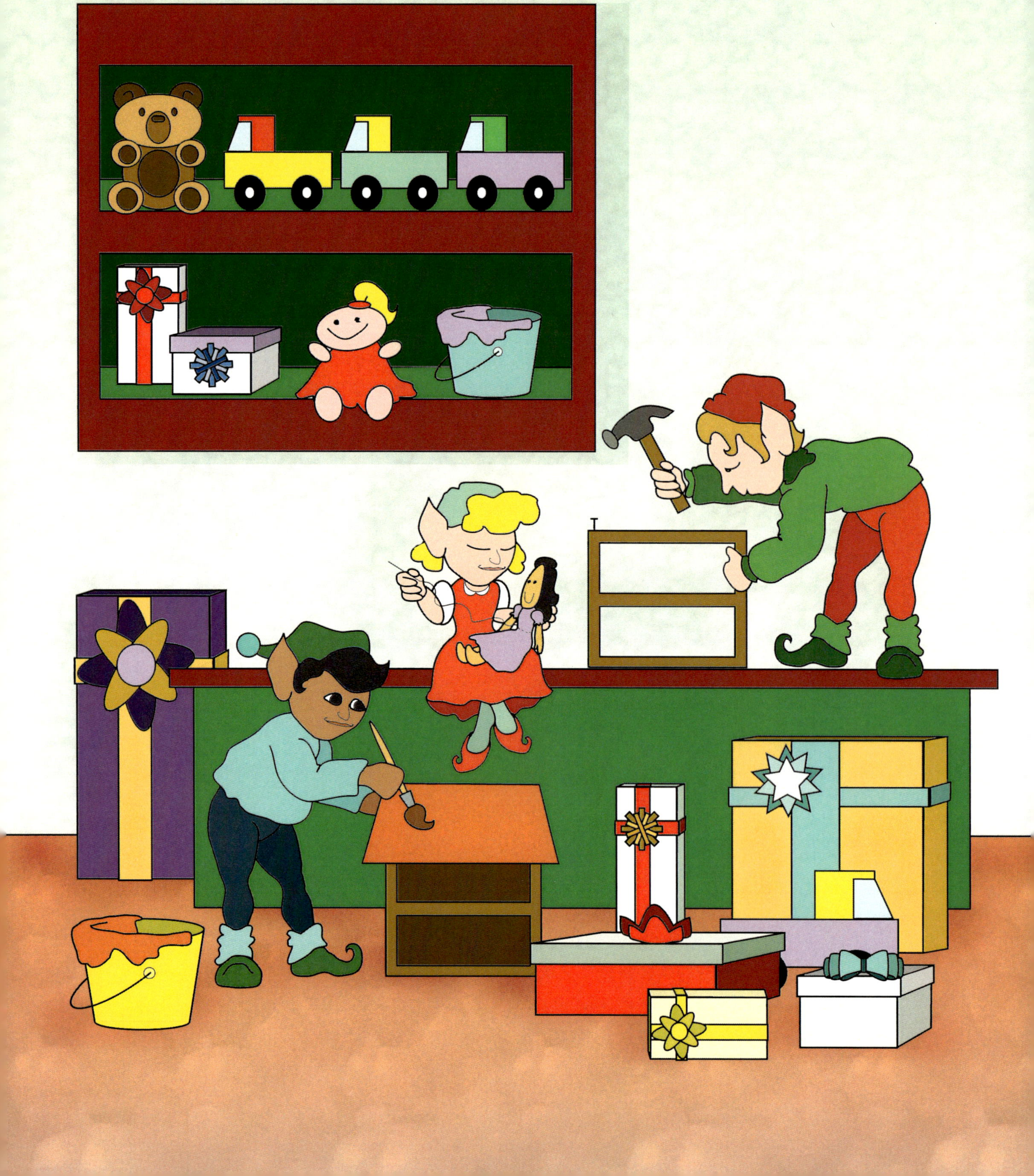

The Elves

The elves, which busy themselves year round building toys, remind us of the church that year round busies itself with giving of the good news of salvation and sharing of all the good things God has done for us.

> *1 Thessalonians 1:2–3 (2) We give thanks to God always for you all, making mention of you in our prayers, (3) remembering without ceasing your work of faith, labor of love, and patience of hope in our Lord Jesus Christ in the sight of our God and Father . . .*

> *Matthew 28:18–20 (18) And Jesus came and spoke to them, saying, "All authority has been given to Me in heaven and on earth. (19) Go therefore and make disciples of all the nations, baptizing them in the name of the Father and of the Son and of the Holy Spirit, (20) teaching them to observe all things that I have commanded you; and lo, I am with you always, even to the end of the age." Amen.*

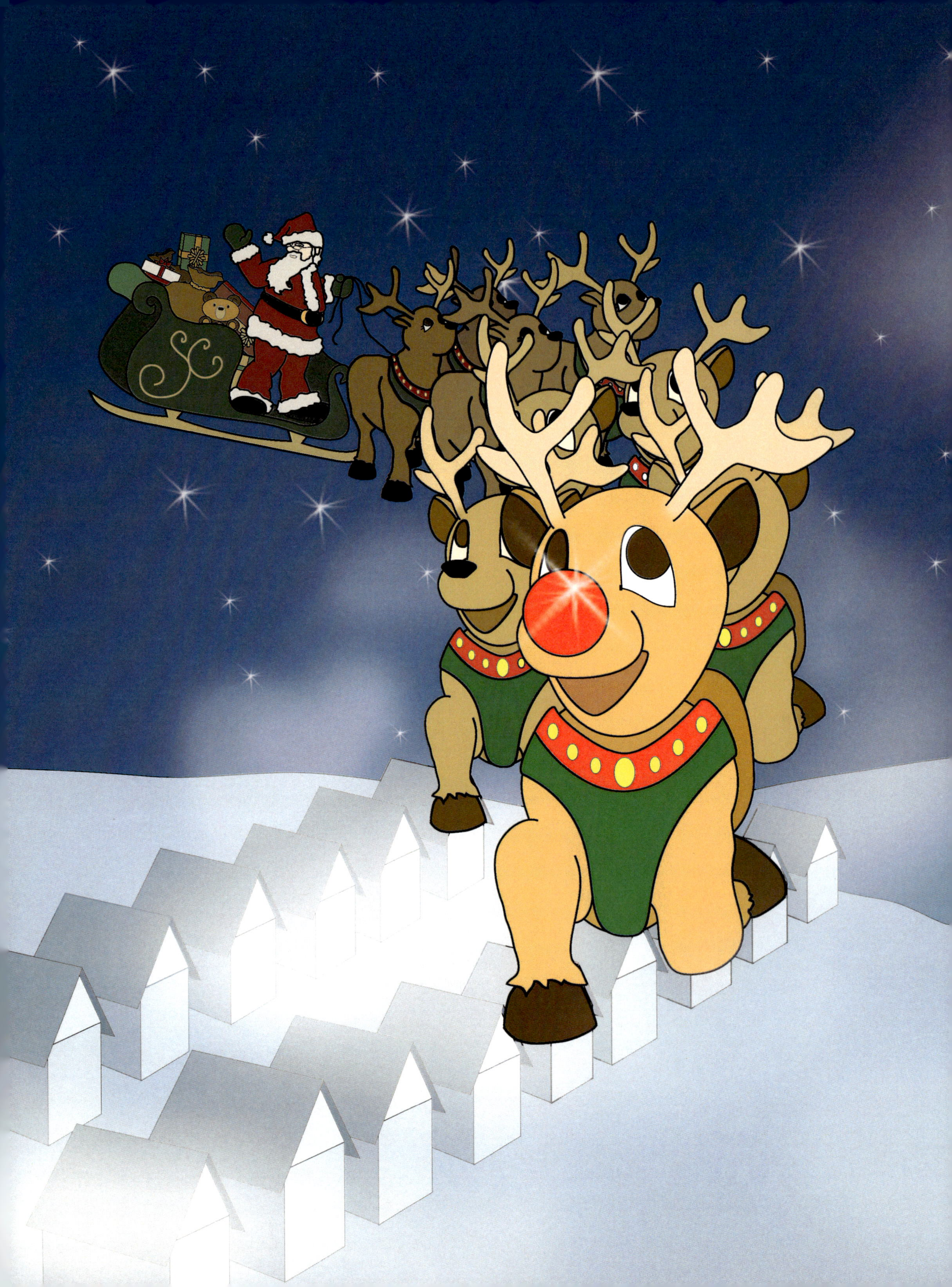

Conclusion

Just as Santa Claus must go to all the world and into every home, so must the news of Christ's coming, death, resurrection, and His coming again go to every part of the world, to every home, and to every heart possible.

ISN'T THAT WHAT CHRISTMAS IS ALL ABOUT?

MY CHRISTMAS PRAYER

Heavenly Father,
I want to thank You for the Christmas tree,
That reminds me of Your love for me.
And under the tree, gifts with ribbons curled,
Remind me Jesus is Your gift to the world.
The colors of Christmas are so bright,
Red, green, blue, yellow, and white.
They tell me about the birth of the King,
Of joy and life that He would bring.
The meaning of Christmas is not just fun,
But Your gift Father–Your precious Son.
Through Him we see Your tender care,
This gift of Jesus nothing can compare.
Father help me this Christmas to see
All that you have done for me.
May all the symbols remind me of You,
And all that Jesus came to do.
Amen.

Leading a Child to Christ

Being a parent, grandparent, or a children's worker is a wonderful opportunity to pass on faith.

Below are some ideas to guide you in leading children to Christ. My goal is that all parents, grandparents, and children's workers will be prepared to lead children to Christ. I hope you will put this information to good use and follow the Holy Spirit as you lead children to Christ. Please consider the following suggestions!

1. **Be sensitive to the leading of the Holy Spirit in the child's life.** Conversion is the work of the Holy Spirit. God will draw children to Himself. Never force, coerce or push children to make a decision. Salvation must be freely accepted.

2. **Understand when the child is ready.** When a child understands that God is a person who loves him or her, when a child can know the difference between right and wrong, when he or she experiences sorrow for doing wrong, and when the child gains a basic understanding of Christ as God's Son who died for his or her sin, then that child is ready to respond to the Lord!

3. **Know how to explain the plan of salvation.** Have a planned presentation of the gospel, but always be ready to adapt it to the child's needs. Encourage the child to ask questions.

Here is a method for presenting the gospel to children.
Jesus wants children to come to Him (Mark 10:14–15).
God loves you and sent Christ to die for you (John 3:16).
You have sinned against God (Romans 3:23).
The penalty for sin is death (Romans 6:23).
You can ask Christ to take away your sins (Romans 5:8).
You can receive the forgiveness of sins (1 John 1:9).
You can become a member of God's family (John 1:12)

4. **Help the child pray to express faith in Christ.** Here is a simple prayer you might use.

"Lord Jesus, I know I have sinned, and I am sorry. I turn away from my sins and ask you to forgive me. I believe you died for my sins. I confess my sins to you, and now I want to receive you into my life as my Friend and Savior. Thank you, Jesus. Amen."

5. **Lead your child into assurance.** Show him or her that he or she will have to keep his or her relationship open with God through repentance and forgiveness (just like with his or her family or friends), but that God will always love him or her ("Never will I leave you; never will I forsake you," Heb. 13:5).

Contact Robert Adams
or order more copies of this book at

TATE PUBLISHING, LLC

127 East Trade Center Terrace
Mustang, Oklahoma 73064

(888) 361 - 9473

Tate Publishing, LLC

www.tatepublishing.com